# RIDING
# THE PROBLEM HORSE

by
Perry Wood

Illustrations by
Carole Vincer

KENILWORTH PRESS

First published in Great Britain by
Kenilworth Press, an imprint of Quiller Publishing Ltd

**British Library Cataloguing in Publication Data**
A catalogue record for this book is available from the British Library

ISBN 1 905693 02 8
    978-1-905693-02-3

Printed in Great Britain by Halstan & Co. Ltd

**Disclaimer of Liability**
The author and publisher shall have neither liability nor
responsibility to any person or entity with respect to any loss or
damage caused or alleged to be caused directly or indirectly by the
information contained in this book. While the book is as accurate as
the authors can make it, there may be errors, omissions and
inaccuracies.

KENILWORTH PRESS
An imprint of Quiller Publishing Ltd
Wykey House, Wykey, Shrewsbury, SY4 1JA
tel: 01939 261616  fax: 01939 261606
e-mail: info@quillerbooks.com
website: www.kenilworthpress.co.uk

# CONTENTS

# INTRODUCTION

Although we all want to ride perfectly well-behaved horses, from time to time most of us find ourselves having to deal with a behaviour problem while riding. These problems can range from bucking and rearing to pulling, shying or bolting. It is not always easy to understand why a horse may be expressing these kinds of behaviours, but if we think about what the root cause may be, it can help us to find a long-term solution that is good for us and for the horse.

It is important to remember that horses are big, strong and fast, and when they show undesirable behaviour under saddle it can be potentially dangerous. This is why it is essential to seek the very best professional help and not try to resolve problems that are beyond our capability.

When a horse misbehaves, it is easy to think it is 'being naughty' or 'playing up', but horses generally want to please us and to have an easy life. They usually show what

we might call 'difficult behaviour' under saddle because of fear, discomfort or pain. Horses have incredible memories, and their behaviour is often triggered by the memory of an unpleasant experience, even after the root cause has been eradicated. If the trigger is an everyday occurrence, the resultant 'bad' behaviour may become a habit.

When a horse exhibits problem behaviour he is trying to communicate something to us. More often than not, he gives small warning signals before behaving 'badly', but we may not notice these, so he communicates in a big way to get his point across. Clever riders therefore pay attention to the horse at all times in order to pick up the early signs of any unwanted behaviour, and intervene to prevent it happening. Smart riders also know that avoidance of a problem makes more sense than having to deal with difficult behaviour or bad habits when riding.

### IMPORTANT

If a horse or pony displays any of the problem behaviours discussed in this book, it is essential to have reputable professionals check the horse's saddle, girth, bridle, teeth and back, before looking at any other causes or courses of action.

Likewise, it is recommended that you seek the help of an experienced professional if your horse or pony exhibits serious behaviour problems or bad habits when ridden.

# DIFFICULT TO MOUNT

Horses can be difficult to mount if they are sore or have a 'cold back', caused by heavy riding, a badly fitting saddle, overwork or physical weakness in the horse's back. Horses that have had a rider's foot dig them in the ribs, or a rider's seat banging down hard or quickly on their back when being mounted, are also likely to be unhappy.

Sometimes this habit occurs because the horse has not been schooled properly or has not been shown what is required.

Horses that do not stand well to be mounted can be in a hurry and this 'hurry' can spill over into their ridden work, making them overly forward-going, too fast or keen to ride.

Don't rush or sit down heavily on the horse's back when you mount.

## Taking action

Whenever possible, use a mounting block; this avoids putting too much weight on one side of the saddle (sometimes causing it to slip) or struggling to mount quickly if the horse moves off before he should.

When teaching the horse to be mounted, a long rope (12ft/3.6m) attached to a halter can be useful, so if he moves away you can easily remain on the mounting block and ask him to come back towards you.

Give yourself plenty of time when teaching a horse to be good to mount – riders often jump into the saddle quickly or get impatient, but a horse that doesn't stand well to be mounted is not truly accepting the rider.

If the horse moves away as you try to mount, quietly bring him back to exactly the

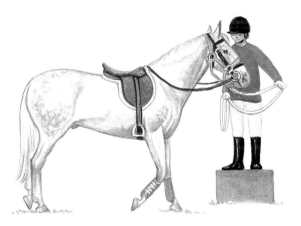

Keep bringing the horse back to the same place until he stands to be mounted. A long rope (12ft/3.6m) attached to a halter can be useful here.

same spot and start again, as many times as necessary. This kind of repetition, done with complete calmness from the rider, is normally sufficient to ultimately produce a horse that is good to mount.

# BUCKING

A classic rodeo-style buck.

A horse that bucks can be unpleasant and difficult to ride. Bucking ranges from the horse lifting his back and kicking his hind legs out for fun, through to the classic rodeo-style buck, where the horse stops moving forwards, drops his head between his front legs and leaps upwards with an arched back. A determined bucking horse requires an extremely competent rider.

There are many causes for bucking: it can be the horse's way of expressing exuberance and *joie de vivre*, but most often it is a sign that the horse is stiff or in physical discomfort.

If a horse bucks through over-excitement, his feeding and exercise regime may need changing. A horse that is confined to the stable or riding arena, fed too much 'heating' grain and not given enough exercise by riding out in the countryside, can become over-excited and buck.

Bucking can often be an expression by the horse that it is having difficulty moving well from behind, so have a professional check the horse for soundness.

## Young horses

Young horses sometimes buck when they become fearful, uncomfortable or confused: they need plenty of time, patience and a slow education, so they can accept each stage of training. If a young horse is rushed into something, whether he is being 'backed', ridden out or is cantering, he may react by bucking.

Punishing a young horse for bucking can upset him and cause more problems, so instead slow down the pace of the training programme and only do things the horse is relaxed and comfortable with.

To find out if the horse is bucking because of the rider, it can help to ask a horse to canter on the lunge. If the horse bucks on the lunge without a rider, he is certainly likely to do so under saddle.

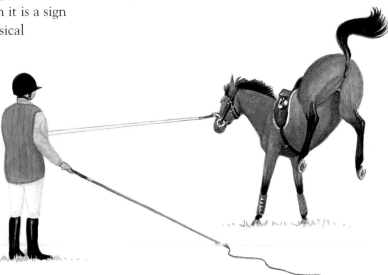

Don't look down
or tip forward.

Look up and ahead, try
to lift the horse's head
upwards with the reins
and ride him briskly
forwards.

## Riding tips

The way we ride can cause a sensitive horse to buck. Tightly gripping legs can make some horses feel uncomfortable in their ribs. If the rider's body is unbalanced, it can upset the horse and cause him to buck. Riders who hold the reins tightly, or who grip or squeeze hard with their legs, can make some horses buck rather than go forwards.

If a horse is more inclined to buck when cantering in the company of other horses or when there are open spaces, begin by getting him used to cantering without bucking in quiet situations, perhaps with another horse present, in the riding arena. Gradually build up to cantering with another horse in open spaces and make sure the other horse doesn't race or overtake your horse.

Some horses only buck when asked for canter. This can be because of stiffness, tension or over-excitement. In this situation it is best to do more work in the slower paces until the horse is more settled and warmed-up before asking for canter.

## Taking action

When a horse bucks he has to slow down, drop his head and arch his back, so an alert rider will lift up a bucking horse's head with one or both reins in a smart upwards action and ride him briskly forwards with the legs.

When a horse bucks, hitting him behind with a stick may make him buck more, but touching him on the shoulder with a stick may help to raise his front while he is bucking.

Make sure you look up, not down. If you look down it is harder to keep your balance; looking up helps you to stay on top and ride the bucking movement going on underneath you.

# REARING

Rearing is when the horse lifts his front legs off the ground and stands up on his back legs. A confirmed rearer is a dangerous animal and should be dealt with by an experienced professional. If a horse rears up high, he can over-balance and fall backwards onto the rider.

## Causes of rearing

The causes of rearing under the rider can be many: some horses rear because they are very sensitive in the mouth and afraid of the feel of the contact on the bit. This can be because they have been ridden in the past by someone with rough hands, or in a bit that is too severe for them.

If a horse is nervous about going out alone or is not confident about riding out, he may become 'nappy' and ultimately rear because he doesn't want to go forwards.

A horse that is held back by strong hands when he is full of impulsion and wants to go forwards may rear, especially if he sees his friends galloping off into the distance without him.

## Taking action

It is best to deal with rearing **before** it happens, and a horse usually gives a few smaller signals or warnings that he is going to rear before he does so – e.g. stopping and refusing to go forwards, lightening his forehand or trying to turn for home.

In order to rear, a horse needs to stop and have his head in front of him. If the rider keeps the horse moving positively forwards it is more difficult for the horse to stop and rear. Alternatively, if the rider bends the horse's head round to one side towards the stirrup **with one rein**, it can interfere with

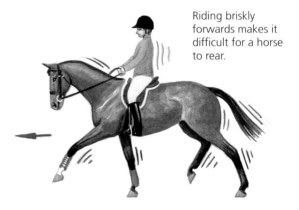

In a rear, try to sit forward and release the rein contact to avoid pulling him over backwards.

A horse finds it more difficult to rear when his head is bent to one side.

Riding briskly forwards makes it difficult for a horse to rear.

the horse's ability to rear.

Once the horse is rearing the rider is fairly powerless to do anything about it. The rider should lean forwards to stay in balance, otherwise the horse may fall backwards or sideways. While the horse rears, the rider can put both arms forwards around the horse's neck and let the reins go slack until the horse's front comes back down to the ground.

# SHYING

Shying or spooking is a natural part of the horse's survival mechanism: horses are prey animals and it is instinctive for them to be looking out for things they think may be a danger, which is why they shy.

## Riding tips

When riding a horse that shies a lot, or when riding a horse past something potentially scary, it is a good idea for the rider to look ahead and ride quietly forwards, rather than getting caught up the horse's spookiness by looking at the offending item.

On approaching a potential 'gremlin', the rider can try turning the horse's head slightly away from the object of its fear, not in an attempt to stop the horse from seeing the object, but to ask him to listen to the rider's aids and positive directions.

If the rider tenses or grips with his legs and/or hands when a horse shies, he gives the horse the message that he (the rider) is also scared, and that the horse's fears are warranted – so it is important for the rider to sit well and stay relaxed when riding a spooky horse.

Do not punish a horse for shying. Do not drive him on with a whip, jab him in the mouth with the reins or kick him hard with the legs, as any of these actions can make him more afraid and associate the object he is shying at with punishment or pain.

Equally, do not pat a horse for passing something he shied at, as he may think he is being rewarded for shying.

Make sure not to over-feed a spooky horse with 'heating' grains, and take him out riding often enough so he is happy about going out into the world without it being a strange and scary place.

## Desensitising

It is possible to gradually desensitise horses to situations or objects which may cause them to spook or shy, e.g. traffic, plastic bags, water, bicycles, etc. To begin with, do this in a safe environment, such as in a riding arena. Start by exposing the horse to tiny amounts of something scary, e.g. scrunch up a refuse bag so it is small, or show it to him from a long distance away, so he is not made to feel afraid.

Progressively increase the horse's exposure to the scary object; do it gradually in a way that maintains his comfort and feelings of being safe. If the horse becomes afraid, make the object smaller or take it further away again. This 'advance and retreat' method should increase the horse's trust in his rider and help him to be less spooky in many situations. (See also Picture Guide 49, 'Bombproofing Tips')

Look straight ahead past the offending object, turn the horse's head and body slightly away from the object, or put him into shoulder-in, and walk him past.

shoulder-in position

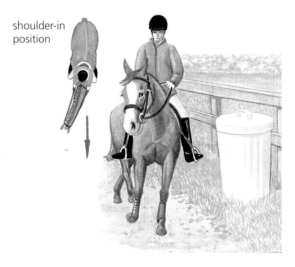

# RUNNING OFF/BOLTING

Horse are 'flight' animals, which means their instinctive reaction is to run away when faced with fear or perceived danger. Of course, a bolting horse will stop running eventually, but in most situations it is not safe to wait until he stops as there isn't normally enough open space to let him run before coming to a road, wall, hedge or other potentially dangerous obstacle.

Horses can also run off or be hard to stop because of over-excitement or lack of schooling, and although this kind of behaviour may seem the same as true bolting, it is easier for the rider to do something about it. Nevertheless, a horse that starts to run off because of excitement or lack of schooling may panic itself into truly bolting, so it is usually a good idea to react appropriately.

## Taking action

The best way to stop a horse from running off is to stop it **before** it goes. Good riders are sensitive to how their horse feels in every moment; they are aware of what he is communicating and how he may react in different situations. Good riders also have quick reactions and good timing, which means they act to stop a horse from gathering strong momentum or too much speed while he is still manageable, preferably within the horse's first 'bolting' stride. As soon as the rider feels the horse going even slightly faster than he wants, or getting inattentive and worried about something, he should take action by bringing the horse back under control through half-halts with one rein or by riding in small circles until he has settled.

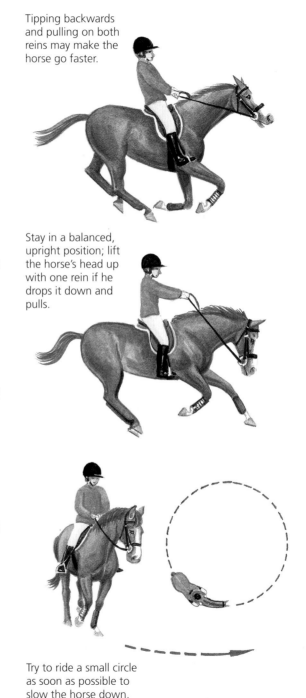

Tipping backwards and pulling on both reins may make the horse go faster.

Stay in a balanced, upright position; lift the horse's head up with one rein if he drops it down and pulls.

Try to ride a small circle as soon as possible to slow the horse down.

## Riding tips

If a horse runs off or bolts, the rider should sit firmly in the saddle, keep his legs **lightly** on the horse's sides, staying upright in the body and looking ahead. One of the most effective ways to respond is to bend the horse's head around with one rein towards the horse's own hip, or to turn the horse in as small a circle as necessary. Both of these actions divert the horse's energy from shooting forwards and make it hard for the horse to keep running away.

If a horse drops his head really low and pulls downwards with his head as he runs, the rider can try putting one hand forward and giving a sharp upward half-halt to lift his head, as well as starting to turn him.

It is important not to expose yourself or the horse to situations in which he may run away. The best way to build the horse's trust, and also your trust in the horse, is to gradually train or re-train him by slowly exposing him to less challenging versions of the situations in which he may run away.

The most common mistake that riders make when a horse runs away is to pull on

Some racehorses are encouraged to go faster by the jockey taking a firm contact on the bit.

both reins: this actually helps the horse to engage his power against them and run more. In fact, many racehorses are encouraged to go faster by their jockeys pulling back and forth on both reins together. Pulling hard on both reins can also make horses run more because in their minds they are trying to run away from the pain or discomfort caused by the bit or the rider's hands.

If your horse speeds up without you asking, bring his speed back down again immediately.

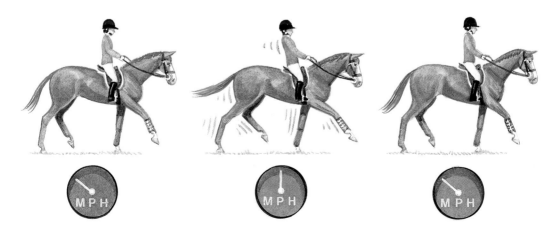

# NAPPING

Napping (or 'jibbing') is where a horse or pony refuses to go forwards, roots himself to the spot, tries to run home, backs up or even rears. This problem is very common because horses are herd creatures; riding out alone is against the horse's natural instinct, because a horse alone in the wild would be a target for predators.

A sensitive rider may feel a horse 'napping' in small ways: e.g. the horse walks faster on the way home than he does on the way out.

A firm rider may push a horse through its nappiness, but if a rider is too strong or insensitive he may actually create or increase the nappy behaviour in a horse. A nervous rider is also likely to make the horse feel insecure and cause nappiness.

A typically nappy horse that doesn't want to leave his home.

## Riding tips

The most important factors in curing or avoiding napping are the level of trust that the horse has in the rider, and schooling the horse to be obedient to the rider's forward aids.

To avoid creating a nappy horse always ride out on circular routes, so that you avoid turning around and coming home by the same route as you went out. Ask for faster gaits (forward trot and canter) on the way out and slower ones on the way home (walk and slow trot).

## Taking action

If the horse is good to lead, casually dismount and lead the horse for a while. It can help the horse to feel reassured by the presence of another being walking with it.

Many horses are nappy when ridden alone and happy when ridden in company; this is

Whenever possible ride out on a circular route, rather than turning round and riding back home the way you went out.

perfectly natural, especially with young horses. Build the horse's confidence by going out with another, reliable horse. Take turns in

If a horse stops dead, wait for as long as it takes to go forwards.

going first for a short while, so that you increase the horse's confidence to go forwards with its nose out in front, especially when going **away** from home.

If a horse stops dead, rather than use more leg, try sitting and 'waiting it out'; allow the horse to stand still or go forwards, but only in the direction you require. Quietly make sure the horse remains facing the direction you want to travel, and occasionally ask him to go forwards with **quiet** leg aids. This technique is good because it doesn't increase the energy or anxiety of the situation and over time builds the horse's trust in the rider. It may require a lot of patience from the rider, who has to be prepared to sit waiting in the same spot, perhaps for hours.

With a horse that spins around towards home or plants his feet on the ground and won't move, turn the horse in very small circles with a loose, open rein. It is fairly easy for the rider to keep the horse on the small circle and stop him from napping for home, and the horse may begin to realise he is not getting anywhere. At this point the rider gives the horse the opportunity to go forwards in a straight line, but only in the direction required by the rider. If the horse again tries to nap, the rider calmly asks for a few more small circles before allowing the horse another opportunity to go forwards. It is essential that the rider stays relaxed, has very quiet legs and asks for the small circles with the reins as loose as possible, while still retaining control.

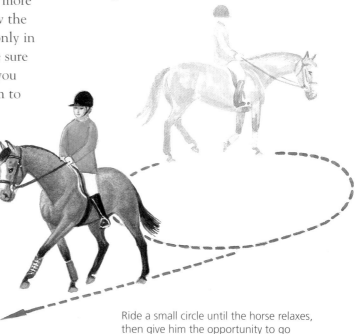

Ride a small circle until the horse relaxes, then give him the opportunity to go forwards, but only in the direction you want.

# NOSE-POKING/STAR-GAZING

When a horse pokes his nose up in the air, or 'star-gazes', he evades the action and control of the bit and can cause himself discomfort through hollowing his back.

It is important to look carefully at what is causing the horse to star-gaze: it could be physical problems with the horse's teeth or back, inappropriate types of bit, the rider sitting badly or being too harsh or rough, the saddle hurting, or a general lack of schooling. Some horses' physical conformation can make them more likely to star-gaze than others.

## Riding tips

A star-gazing horse needs to be ridden very sensitively and re-schooled over an extended period of time (usually months) to learn to carry himself without throwing his head up.

When a horse star-gazes, the rider should soften his body, seat, back and hands. If the rider sits heavily or causes discomfort to the horse, the horse's back will hollow and, as a consequence, the head goes up.

## Taking action

With a nose-poker, it is essential that the rider avoids pulling both reins together, because when a horse star-gazes he braces the muscles through his back and neck, and pulling both reins together increases the bracing of these muscles. In contrast, if the rider asks the horse to flex or bend his head a little to one side, the horse can begin to let go and drop his nose.

Yielding forwards a little with the hands sometimes helps a star-gazing horse to let go and lower his head.

Make sure you keep your legs in **light** contact with the horse.

Riding curves or circles, rather than straight lines, helps the nose-poking horse to unlock the brace in his neck and back, eventually helping him to relax and drop his head down.

Avoid heavy or strong riding, especially with your hands or seat.

Ride in nice, light balance with a quiet seat, hands and legs.

# REFUSING TO JUMP

Horses who refuse to jump have usually had a bad experience of jumping some time in their past. If anyone pulls them in the mouth, bangs down on their back or loses their temper and punishes them when jumping, the horse will soon dislike or fear jumping.

Horses are very sensitive to the rider's emotions, so if the rider has any doubts about a jump, the horse may well refuse. It is essential not to lose your temper when jumping, as this will soon put the horse off.

Make sure the horse is not refusing to jump because of physical pain or discomfort.

## Riding tips

It helps the horse by approaching the jump straight: try having wings either side of the jump or forming a small jumping lane.

Set up a very small jump (about 1ft/30cm high) in the riding arena and **ask the horse to jump it only once**, at the very end of your riding session, then dismount, feed him and put him away. If this is done each time you ride, in a short while the horse may start wanting to go over the jump because he knows it will lead to a reward. Once he is thinking that way, you can gradually ask him to jump more.

Make sure you time your jumping seat with his stride, sit softly with good hands, and give him his head at the right moment. Focus beyond the jump, rather than look at it.

## Poles

Start training or re-training a horse to jump in very small ways, using trotting poles or cavaletti, so the horse slowly becomes accustomed to it.

When introducing a small jump, try placing a pole on the ground about 9ft/2.7m in front of the obstacle, to help the horse take the correct stride into the jump. Begin by using a small jump made up of two cross-poles, so the middle is very low; this is inviting and trains the horse to go for the centre of jumps.

Use a very small obstacle to encourage the horse to jump.

# JOGGING

Jogging is when a horse potters along with shortened trot steps rather than walking out properly. Jogging is usually a form of mental tension in the horse, perhaps anxious about getting home or keeping up with his friends. It can also be the result of the horse not having a naturally ground-covering walk and trying to trot instead.

## Riding tips

Riding jogging horses is a delicate matter. They can become very collected and overly sensitive to the rider's leg and rein aids: too much leg may cause them to jog even more or run away, and too much rein may cause them to over-collect and rear, so it is important to be **very** relaxed and light with all the aids. If the rider gets tense, constantly nags with the legs and/or holds the horse tight with the reins, this can encourage a horse to jog more.

Because jogging is habit-forming, it is important not to let the horse jog for a while before bringing it back to walk, as the horse may think it is OK to jog. It is the rider's job to stop a horse from jogging and it is best if the rider is very clear and consistent that the horse either walks or does a proper trot.

## Taking action

When a horse jogs, try asking him to yield his head and neck softly a few degrees to one side by lightly opening one rein. This slows the horse and lowers his neck, causing him to drop into a walk. Most likely he will only walk for a stride or two before jogging again, but quiet persistence from the rider will extend the time the horse walks until he

Jogging can become an engrained habit that takes time and patience to cure.

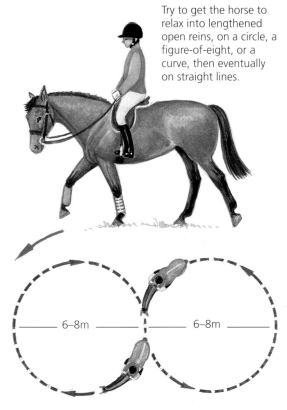

Try to get the horse to relax into lengthened open reins, on a circle, a figure-of-eight, or a curve, then eventually on straight lines.

6–8m     6–8m

Try to ride a small figure-of-eight and wait for the horse's energy level drop.

finds it easier to stay in a swinging walk.

If there is plenty of space, ask the horse to go in small circles or figures-of-eight (two 6–8m circles joined together), with the reins as slack as possible. This teaches the horse that he can use his excess energy but doesn't actually go anywhere. This pattern also loosens the horse's body, relaxing and suppling the muscles he needs in order to walk in a more effective and swinging way.

Avoid riding out with other excitable horses as they may make your horse jog more.

When a horse drops from a jog to a walk, even for a stride or two, do not try pushing him into walking faster, as he will probably start jogging again.

Ride out with another horse that is quiet, steady and reliable. This is more helpful than riding in the company of other high-energy horses, as they affect each other and increase the tendency to jog.

If your horse leads well, try dismounting and leading him for a while, as this sometimes helps him feel less anxious.

Remember that horses get excited by anything new, so if they only go out occasionally they are more likely to get excited and jog.

Choose a quiet companion horse to ride out with to help your horse relax in his walk.

Make sure the horse is not stabled too much of the time and not fed too much high-energy food.

Ultimately, proper schooling of the horse to teach him to walk, trot and canter at the speed of the rider, in response to the rider's leg, rein, seat and voice aids should cure a jogger.

# HEAD-TOSSING

This can be a difficult problem to resolve, as there are many reasons for its occurrence and it is not always easy to know which particular one is the cause.

Horses may head-toss because they are sore in the mouth, their teeth need attention, they have pain in the back, their hindquarters are weak, the saddle is uncomfortable, the bit is hurting, the rider's hands or seat are too harsh, they lack proper schooling, or are allergic to something in the air, such as pollen.

## Taking action

Look at the way the horse is being ridden: does the rider have a soft seat and good hands? Some head-tossing horses will not show this behaviour with a quiet rider.

Try different bridles, such as a kind hackamore; remember that a hackamore is designed to be used mostly with loose reins, without a 'constant contact'.

A skilful, quiet rider can try putting the head-tossing horse on the bit with soft hands and a good seat. It is very important that the rider doesn't fiddle or be over-active with the hands or legs.

School the horse on circles and figures-of-eight, rather than on straight lines; this encourages the horse to stretch his head forwards and down, so improving his back muscles.

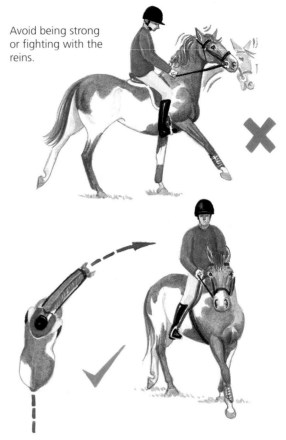

Avoid being strong or fighting with the reins.

Ride the horse on a soft rein on circles or curves; the arc of the circle helps the horse to settle his head.

hackamore bitless bridle

nose net

snaffle bit with plastic mouthpiece

Softer bits, such as rubber or plastic (left), or a bitless hackamore (above), may work with some horses; and if head-tossing happens at certain times of the year (perhaps caused by seasonal allergies or fly problems), try a net nose-cover, available from saddlery shops.

# OVER-EXCITABLE

People often think that an over-excitable horse is having fun or enjoying itself, but this kind of behaviour often stems from tension, anxiety or apprehension.

## Taking action

If a horse is kept stabled, avoid over-feeding with heating grains and take him out riding regularly.

Avoid placing the horse in situations where he becomes excitable until he has been taught to trust his rider, relax under saddle and listen to the aids. Give the horse lots of quiet work in the slower paces (walk and an occasional slow trot). It is not always a good idea to 'work him through it' by pushing on in strong trot and canter in the hope of taking the edge off him or tiring him – many horses have huge amounts of stamina and when over-excited will sometimes keep running despite being exhausted.

Slowly expose the horse to small examples of whatever triggers the over-excitement. For example, if the horse becomes excited in company, go for a short ride (maybe even only a few yards) with a very quiet companion horse. If the problem arises at shows, try taking the horse to some very small local shows, and just ride or lead him around for a while then take him home, without entering a class.

## Riding tips

If you find yourself on an over-excited horse, avoid being strong with the reins or legs, as this can lead to more tension in the horse and even cause him to be more explosive. It is a good idea to have a light leg contact with the horse, rather than taking the legs

Over-excited horses are often anxious or afraid.

away from him.

If there is space, put him onto a pattern of small circles or a small figure-of-eight. This gives his excess energy an outlet and enables him to keep moving, but also means you have more control. Continue to ride the pattern until the horse becomes calm, which may take some time.

Have a soft rein contact so you can guide the horse effectively on the pattern without having to tug him around and wind him up even more. Whenever the horse slows, relaxes or drops his head, reward him with your voice and by softening your body.

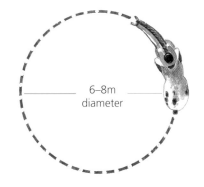

6–8m
diameter

Redirect the horse's energy by putting him onto a small circle until he calms down.

# HARD-MOUTHED

Hard-mouthed horses can be tiring to ride and difficult to control. The reasons for a horse being hard-mouthed are numerous, but with skilful training or re-training it is possible to lighten most horses' mouths to some degree.

Horses that have been ridden with strong hands or forced into an outline are almost inevitably going to end up hard-mouthed; the horse's mouth is sensitive but can become numb through harsh or inexperienced riding.

Remember that horses need to be trained to 'have a mouth' and that it is not natural for them to understand what the bit means without being taught.

## Taking action

Many horses only become hard-mouthed in certain situations, e.g. when they are excited or nervous. Sympathetic riders notice when and where their horse becomes hard in the mouth, avoid those situations and then re-train the horse, gradually re-introducing him to the problem situations in small chunks. For example, if the horse becomes more hard-mouthed when riding out in company, go out with only one other, quiet horse and stay in walk, with maybe a little trot when heading away from home. Progress to riding out in the company of more horses, and quicken the paces. The process may take weeks or even months, but it is essential that the horse stays light and responsive to your hands.

Another cause of horses being hard-mouthed is physical stiffness in the horse's body, particularly in the hindquarters, due to old age, lack of training, wear and tear from overwork or conformation. **Stiffness in a horse's body almost always shows in the mouth**.

Pulling back with both reins is not the best way to deal with a hard-mouthed horse.

If re-schooling a hard-mouthed horse, avoid situations where he is inclined to pull.

## Schooling/re-schooling

Many hard-mouthed horses are not actually hard in the mouth, rather they are too strong, stiff or locked in their neck, which makes them feel strong on the reins. The remedy for this is to soften the horse's neck by regular gentle flexing of the head and neck. This can be done initially from the ground and then in the saddle in halt and later in walk – gently and slowly tease the horse's head around towards one side, then repeat on the other side.

When asking the horse to respond lightly to the reins, use one rein more than the other, as this means the horse can only be half as strong as when both reins are used simultaneously. (Of course, don't always use the same rein.)

Teach the horse to lead impeccably and to back-up lightly using a halter from the ground, and then progress to using a bit – **a horse that reins back lightly will become lighter in the mouth.**

To help a hard-mouthed horse become lighter, try to improve your riding; if the rider's legs, body or hands are stiff, strong or tight, the horse may pull harder against the reins.

From the ground, teach the horse to yield backwards softly.

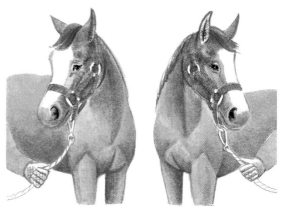

Also from the ground, train him to be flexible and soft in his neck by asking him to yield his head to either side.

From the saddle, teach him to yield his head softly to each side.

# Not Listening/Inattentive

When a horse doesn't listen to his rider he is more likely to act on his flight instinct and shy, nap or run away, so the effective rider always asks the horse to listen and pay attention.

## How do you know he's not listening?
The early warning signs that a horse is not listening to his rider are the position of the head and ears, which point in the direction of his attention, e.g. if he is turning his head or ears to the left, he is probably focusing on something over to the left and not thinking about his rider.

## Riding tips
It is good practice to teach the horse to pay attention firstly when he is being led, and then under saddle.

When he is being led or ridden and he looks away, use the rope or rein to quietly direct his head back to the middle, or very slightly towards you. When the horse is listening, you will feel him release the tension in his neck and the rein, as if saying, 'Yes, I'm with you.' If he looks away again, calmly repeat the process, and in time he will become more attentive and lighter to your requests. The aim is to have the horse listening without you having to hold him there.

In an arena, if the horse is more interested in what is going on elsewhere, ride him with a slight flexion of his head to the inside of the school, so he always looks very slightly into the arena.

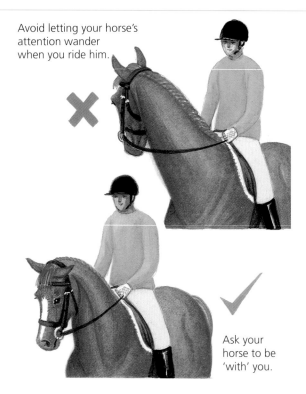

Avoid letting your horse's attention wander when you ride him.

Ask your horse to be 'with' you.

If a horse is really distracted and not listening to you, try keeping him busy with changes of direction, turns and transitions in quick succession; that way he has less time to think about his own agenda and instead has to concentrate on what you are asking him to do.

# LYING DOWN

Horses sometimes lie down with a rider when they are tired or hot and itchy on their backs. Some horses resort to lying down if they have been over-faced, over-ridden or beaten in the past, since this is their way of 'giving up'. A horse in this state is very sad indeed and will need lots of kindness and understanding if it is to trust a rider again.

Some horses lie down with one rider but not with another. The rider who avoids the problem keeps the horse 'awake', going smartly forwards and listening to his rider; the rider with whom the horse lies down lets the horse lose concentration, so much so the horse forgets he is being ridden.

## Taking action

If a horse lowers himself to lie down, the rider needs to use his legs and possibly a stick to ask the horse to go briskly forwards, and simultaneously raise the horse's head with the reins. The voice can also encourage the horse to stay up and move on.

With a horse that lies down because he is 'giving up' as a result of harsh treatment, it is important to remain calm and quiet, and work on gradually rebuilding the horse's trust in humanity again.

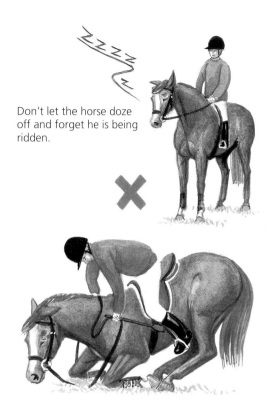

Don't let the horse doze off and forget he is being ridden.

If the horse attempts to lie down, avoid looking down or losing balance.

Lift the horse with the reins, ride him forward with your legs or stick, and try using your voice to ask him to get back up.

23

# CONCLUSION

This book highlights some of the many ways in which we can experience problems with a riding horse's behaviour but, as we have seen, there is usually a good explanation for it if we are aware of the horse's natural instincts and fears. It always helps us to understand things from the horse's point of view – to ask ourselves why the horse feels the need to express itself through certain difficult behaviour – so that we are in a good position to help ourselves and the horse resolve the problem together.

Of course, there are times when something happens unexpectedly when riding, and it is helpful to have some tips and techniques to deal safely with the horse's problem behaviour in that moment. But horses are big, strong and fast, so it is important to think about solutions and seek professional help whenever necessary, rather than risk our own safety or upset the horse further by fighting him or trying to force an issue.

As long as we remember that horses need plenty of time, patience and skill, as well as an understanding of their nature, we can overcome many ridden problems, making riding safer and more enjoyable for ourselves and our horses.